LIFE

LIFE

Sabrina Gregory

much Love

Sabrina Gregory

To order additional copies of this book, contact:
Xlibris Corporation
1-888-795-4274
www.Xlibris.com
Orders@Xlibris.com
71498

CONTENTS

Anger That I Feel

Anger that grows within me.
My aura is not clean.
It grows and grows within me.
I don't know why I'm holding on to so much grief.
My blood boils; my fuse is short and ready.
Can you see the flames growing within me?

Anger keeps building and I don't know how to stop it.
My heart is dark. My feet feels the heat.
Making a way to a calm place.
I'm scorned, I'm mad.
Can you help a sad person trying to come back?
Coming back to the place I once knew.

Anger that I feel strong and steamy.
The energy that I waste can not be retrieved.
It's rolling down the river, lost in the waves.
I tried therapy, I tried group.
Nothing seems to work, not even praying on my knees.

I see myself walking off the edge.
But the voices within says "No."
Can someone see that I'm crying out for help?
Screaming and yelling, no one is there to hear me.
Drowning in anger, feeling pain and I need no sympathy.

I'm trying to find a quite place where I can be free.
Living with anger is so difficult, can't you see?
Making my way to a hand, that's held out for me.
Crossing the street to a kind face that I recognized in the crowd.

You helped me see that my anger can be set free. Hold my hand and watch it go away, so easy you can see. My anger was an excuse to release all the frustration in me. So hard to live with the day to day routine. So I have to find a solution to this anger that's within me. Go away you dark cloud that hovers over me.

Fly away like an eagle and set me free.

<u>Being Alone With Myself</u>

Sometimes I can hear myself thinking. Alone in a hallow space. The sounds of nothing is befitting. It gets so bad that the thought of being by myself is a nightmare. Sometimes I can hear someone whispering my name like maybe a ghost is in the room with me.

Thus, I let my inner voice speak louder so that I can hear over the city streets, loud horns and traffic jams. Living in a town that never sleeps, one can loose themselves in all the hype. Lost my self-esteem a long time ago. I'm not a sell out or hypochondriac. Friends that are dear to me are always there. I'm an only child with such a great bond with my mom. Yes! I'm a mama's girl.

No dad issues, just lack of confidence. Was not voted the pretties girl in high school or most likely to succeed. Did very well in sports. I guess the tomboy side of me tried so hard to be liked by all. After awhile I just decided to be myself and dammed anyone who did not like me. That was a hard role to play out.

Home alone is how I feel right now. Don't you hate when you call a friend and they say "Hey, I was just about to call you, you read my mind or that old dumb line I lost your number." What a croak of bologna. So that meant that I was not important enough for you to save my number.

So now I'm alone. No disappointments, no missed appointments, no lost numbers, or any hurt because people did not show up. Don't care if they come late to my private party. No one can hurt me anymore.

Can I Get Thru The Week

Can I get thru each day that the kids are home for the week? No rest in site. Making more meals than I can count. Can I watch a show without interruptions? Can I hear myself think in a loud house? Can I have a moment of peace, when the kids are around?

Making it through the day without pulling out of my hair. Trying to get my husband to take advantage of these precious moments. Sneak a kiss or take a walk around the block. Can't he see that mom needs some quiet time. The kids have all of the fun while mommy works relentlessly from dusk till dawn. Just thinking only of the fun they are having.

Can't I take a shower without a knock at the door for something that could wait? Can the week go any faster so that I can rest? The days are long and the nights are short. Not enough sleep or rest.

The middle of the week means Friday is just a couple of days away. The kid's get nervous because the fun is almost over. Back to doing homework. Their rooms are a mess. The crunch time on Sunday to get things done, like the neglected homework. Relaxation and fun has come to an end.

Getting thru the week is just a couple of hours. Can't where is that damn bus? Why is it late? Oh, I can see that yellow bus turning the corner. Go faster bus, I can't wait for the bus doors to open. Giving each child a kiss on their forehead, I rushed back into the house to sit down and have a quiet cup of coffee. Finally, a few quiet moments without the rug rats under foot.

Can I have A Moment Of Your Time?

Can I have a moment of your time?
Just a minute or two.
Time enough to talk till we are blue in the face.
Catch a glimpse of the blue sky in the middle of June.

Can I have a moment of your time?
Time to know what's on your mind.
Time to count the ripples on your forehead when things are hot and heavy.
Time to catch you in the mood.
Catch you in that moment to watch that frown turn upside down.

Can I have a moment of your time?
Touch your flesh, to see your soul and explore your mind.
Can I have a moment of your time?
To love you till the very end of time.

Truth

See the truth and feel the cold from the eyes of a blind man's soul. Many people will call you a wimp and call you insane but the reality is you have to make your own fate. Look within yourself and temp fate. Make your own trail and don't be afraid to walk on the untraceable path to your future success.

If everyone's path were the same, the world would be a boring place. Never give up on yourself. Take a challenge, push yourself to the limit. Dare to be successful and unique.

To all of the people who did not believe in you ha ha! To the teacher who said that you did not have potential, kiss it! You are king or queen of your castle and ruler of your destiny.

Can I Help You?

It seems that everyone needs help these days from the government and that includes me. The homeless shelter are packed. The poor needs money and the rich stays on top of the world. CEO's of big firms takes advantage thus forcing these struggling companies into bankruptcy.

All I want to do is to help my family. Being sick all the time has made me a victim. Staying at home has made a hermit. The only time I leave the house is to go the doctor's office, therapy weekly, shopping, cleaning, doing the laundry and guarding over my little's one each day as I take them back and forth to school. Going to so many different doctors has made me hate going. Every time I go they find something else wrong or add a new pill to take for this and that.

Can you help me you figure out what is wrong with me. When you stay at home not by choice you become a prisoner. Your children and your husband forget that you are in pain each day. Forget you are sick and tired of being sick and tired. They forget how to clean up after themselves. Leaving dishes in the sink, clothes laying around for you to pick up, floors dirty from spills and room uninhabitable unless you straighten them up.

Can you help?

Cheaters

If I take you through the forest could you find your way back. This is a decision some people have to make. If I led you to the tree of forbidden fruit would you be tempted to take a bite. Taking the risk, breaking the rules.

Fool me once shame on you. Fool me twice then I'm a fool. A fool in love is a shameful sight. The signs were always there and I refused to see. The condoms in the car, the hang ups when I answered the phone, the cell phone you left off when you do come home, the panties that I found that were two sizes too small that miraculously disappeared because you knew you had cheated.

Cheaters are selfish and have no respect for anyone. They only do what makes them feel good. Lack of respect for other and the art of deception is a quick fix. Cheaters can look you dead in your eyes and swear they are telling the true. The lies just flow thru without a blink of an eye. Telling one lie after another. Losing sleep over how you feel will never happen. The choices are clear and your mind is made up. Shall I stay or shall I go. It's a choice that's made in a split second. The denial, the do I forgive him or the debate with yourself, "should I stay or should I go." Stay strong in order to make this inevitable decision. Your heart just can't take it. Your heart is weak from all of the stress you are under. Look in the mirror and say it over and over again and again. **I REFUSE TO BE A DOORMAT EVER AGAIN!**

Clearing Your Mind and Soul

Cleaning your house and getting rid of the things you don't need or want, I've made my life much easier. In my daily living I have done the same thing. Not letting the clutter block my way. Keeping a clear path. Getting rid of the negativity and replacing it with someday positive.

Making a list and sticking to it makes shopping for your items less complicated. Jot down a realistic list of things you would like to do and accomplish. Go down the list one by one and by the time you have finish you will feel better.

Clearing your soul is just as easy. Clearing you mind eliminating doubt. Feel proud of yourself and pat yourself on the back every once in a while. Your sanity is where peace lies. Your sanity helps bring back the internal freedom that makes good things happen to you. LIVE YOUR LIFE TO THE FULLEST. Enjoy each day to the fullest. Laughter and loving life clears your mind and soul of all those crazy thoughts. Clean out the closet, rid yourself of all the cluster thus starting a new life of peace and joy.

Dear Buddy:

Hi, it's me, Sabrina, I'm writing this letter to thank you for all the help you have given to me and my family. The help came when we really needed it. Facing rough times, with no help in sight, it was nice to know that you had our back. Thank you for your generosity.

You did not forget your family and you knew that we all had fallen on hard time. Desperate for relief. Trying to get from under the disparity. You became our savor and my hero.

I remember when I was a child you made the simplest things fun. Taking care to include all the family members and made sure we knew that you gave a dam. Please do not change. Don't turn into the Jones's. Keep your heart open. Forever sharing wisdom to all.

An elephant never forgets, a snake will bite you without warning, a fox will eat your chickens in the hen house just because he can but I know you will never let any harm come to us.

We are a tribe and you are our leader. Never letting your wealth and it's power change your free will. Be on the lookout for us. Standing guard at all times.

Don't forget the hard times, just a flip of a coin can change your life in a instance. Stay humble, walk a straight path, stay away from the evils of the world. Don't let temptation take over your gracious ways.

Straight from the heart; Sabrina Gregory

Dear John:

I thought that I should write you a letter to end this relationship. The constant calling and harassment is out of control. We have tried to no avail to work out this relationship for many years. We have come to the fork in the road. Dead end is how one can describe it. I'm being stalked by you. I move and you find me, change my phone number and you find a way to get the new number. I'm afraid to pick up the phone in my own home for fear of hearing you on the other end. I've even tried to block my number that won't work. You try to disguise your voice, like I don't recognize your voice after all these years of your hounding me.

Just go away and find another woman to harass. So many times I tried to settle our disputes. You just want budge. You have taken money from the bank account, stolen my income tax check and caused me to go insane. I even tried having a open relationship to get you off of my back, letting the other woman deal with you. Give me a breather. I guess I have to result to paying you off in hopes of never seeing you again.

My bills are piling up. So now I am writing this Dear John letter to end this mess. Don't call me anymore, don't write, just loose my number and address. Goodbye!!!!!

Your settled account;
Sabrina Gregory, paid in full

My Desperate Ho's

My desperate Ho's, they live in the projects and they had very unusual names, Shatasha, Gonarea, and Rashintheass. They were very popular, in the hood. Several times a week the three women got together and played spades. The Kool-Aid was spiked and the kids played in the needle infected park after 7p.m. No one gave a good shit about the kids or their moms.

Shatasha had a good job at the supermarket getting down on her knees for the boss. Gonaera worked at the school cleaning toilets and Rashintheass worked at the free client giving out condoms to the pimps. Their pads were on the third floor in the project of Rejects.

They loved to watch All My Children and they loved that show because it gave them a chance to watch the rich white people have problems. On Monday they all sent their kid's to school. Their kids names were Nickelbag, Razar, Slimjim, Coldcash and Spitbeforushallow. Nickelbag was the oldest and he was in charge of taking everyone to school. He was the smartest kid who repeated the eighth grade for the third time, he knew the streets well because this was his stomping ground to hustle for the dollar bills.

Gonarea had just cashed her welfare check and the school always gave her the leftover chilly on Wednesday's. Rahintheass never had no money but she hustled the pimps for change. Shatasha always had food in her house cause the man in the supermarket gave Shatasha food for going down on knees each week. Don't tell his wife cause she already kicked him out once. The word on the street was all three of these women knew how to play their game. When a nigger asked "DO YOU NEED ANY MONEY?' Their answer was hell yeah. The women's deadbeat dads never gave a dam. No husbands, no headache, more sex for less money was the rule. Play a man, sing the song – in the end you find another sucker to take his place.

Since this is not a T.V show like All My Children but a real life show where everyone gets laid and received something in return. This show is sad but true can you blame a girl. Too many children and no money in site. A women got to do what she has to do. Like sell her ass on Monday to get food for the rest of week.

Sad but true in the hood. A rough place where no one gives a damn. The white people live uptown so that they don't have to come downtown and get cut. The #4 train make express stops downtown. Straight to the poor house, you do not pay the toll. Rasintheass tried to be a good girl at on time. Straight night to five, what did that get her. Children Service took her children away because she was at work and the kids where left alone. The kids tried to cook her dinner in the oven with newspapers and matches. That ended badly because they almost burned down the projects. So from that day on she played it close to the edge without being illegal. What one don't know won't hurt no-one.

Gonerea tried to be legal but it never worked, so she played niggers for every dime they had. She just made it look good by working part time at the school. Gonerea got burned long time ago so in her mind when you play with fire you get burned. Gonerea had a disease that ended her baby making days. So the five kid's she had was all she could ever have. Gonerea always wanted ten kids so that she could be on welfare for life. A ghetto goal for a ghetto minded girl. Not all things were kool aide and ice cream. The rough times brought about drastic changes in the hood. The liquid store no longer sold liquor on Sundays. Trading food stamps to your friends for the value in cash so that you could get your drug stash for a later day or after church on Sunday. Oh yes, they went to church, how else could they find the preachers in the confessional and the gangsters that came to church on Sunday with their families to praise God. Meeting the feel me now's and prayer later. This was the desperate HO's way of living in the hood. Same shit, different day, different time, different place.

Don Forman

Don Forman is in a class all by himself. A loving and caring soul. An angel sent from heaven. All the words in the world cannot describe him. When I first met Don I was a mess. My self esteem and confidence was very low. Walking with my head hanging down. The stress of life and my health issues had me in a depressive state. Now in just seven months I'm a much better person not totally fixed in my head but I'm looking at things in a different light.

Taking one day at a time, being myself and not letting the world sit on my shoulders. Living each day as me and not letting anyone rain on my parade. I'm doing whatever it takes to improve myself. With a little help with drugs and therapy, I'm healing from within.

Don Forman came into my life as my Savor. He helped me get back on track. Going to group is therapeutic. Trying never to miss. I thought I could never do this because of my pride that stood in the way. Never say never. This was the hardest thing I ever had to do. Fitting in with a group of strangers, spilling my guts. Group session makes me feel better. I needed the groups help to see me though. Just remember your problems become small after hearing the other persons inhabitations. They too need your help.

Looking back at Don's problems and his overwhelming grief from losing his son and dealing with his wife's scary moment with cancer, I then realized how strong of a man he was. I truly had all the respect in the world for him. He never once gave in or showed us his disparity nor did he miss work because of these personal issues. Just like us he stood tall and put his personal problems behind him and gave us his strong shoulder to lean on. Always there when we needed him.

Don, we tip our hats to you. You deserve a metal and we raise our glass to a man that has given us good and sound advise from the heart. A true friend, and an excellent therapist.

Don you have changed my life for the better and I could not have found a better man to help me thru my troubled times. Thank you, Don Forman, for bringing me back to reality.

Finding Myself

I looked in the mirror and I saw a stranger. I felt lost after all these years. My marriage in shambles, working and struggling to raise my kids was devastating. The harsh reality of life had set in. With life so hard and difficult my frame of mind had changed. My self esteem was gone. My outlook on life has changed and my mind is foggy. I had to step back and change some things in order to go on.

From almost dying in the hospital to having a total nervous breakdown. I knew something had to change. Everything seemed to be against me. I had to take control. No more ducking and dodging the bullet.

Can things change? Taking another look into the mirror again and saying this time I will get it right. Improving my daily thoughts in order to make a better me. Have to find myself. Challenging and making myself ready for a fresh start. Stepping up to the plate and taking that first swing, one strike at a time. Remembering to make a home run. You go girl—you are on the path to success.

Putting myself into therapy. Talking out my problems. Healing my inner soul a little at a time. Now for the first time I looked into the mirror and I saw the real me. The smile is back. Thirty nine and fabulous. For the first time I'm wearing make-up and I'm on the path to a becoming a better person.

Flip Side

Looking for the silver lining is all around us, one just needs to find it.
The sun will rise and shine for us if we believe.
The sun and the moon is a controlling factor which controls our waking up and our time to rest. The days longer and the nights too short.

The silver lining is there for the taking. Be ever so thankful for food to eat and a warm bed in which to sleep.
Living in this cruel world is not all bad. We still have so much to be thankful for.

The good will someday be able to reap the fruits of their labor. Able to be on top of the world. Able to finally be free at last of the ball and chains that held them down.
Remembering that our great leaders died in pursuit of our freedom.
Life is worth living in spite of the storms we face.

Flip side of the bad is always good. Forever marching victoriously for peace. Behind every good man or woman there is a super hero emerging.

Getting Over It

When times are rough don't get even, get over it. There is a silver lining at the end of the rainbow. It can't get any worst, it can only to get better. I know from experience. Yes, the bad times seem to last longer than the good. But with perseverance one can overcome all obstacles.

Don't jump off that ledge yet. Come back. Wake up and make a plan for yourself. Find out what you need to do to get back on the right track. Let it rain and clear it out. Get past the difficult times. Those difficult times make you a stronger person in the future.

Let all that positive energy take over. Let all that negativity go. Staying positive is your winning ticket. Getting past it and moving on. Make a promise to yourself. Never give in, fight back and do not bury your head in the sand. Keep your head up high.

Girl Wake Up!!!

Wake up girl. Open your eyes and see the truth. Life doesn't revolve around your fake ass.
Wake up and take that mirror from your hands, your makeup is great.
Wake up there's more to you than those tits and ass.
They are just superficial—just an added plus that don't mean a thing.
Wake up girl, the flowers are not just for you, they may be for someone else.
Wake up girl don't fall asleep under the hair dryer. The weekly visits are costing you a small fortune.
Stop the madness and get over yourself.
Females need to learn they are not just a piece of ass or a troupe wife, we can do anything we put our mind too.
Girl just wake up before it's too late because your looks fades.
Don't let the real world pass you by.

Good News

Good morning, good afternoon and good night. Should I give you the good news first or the bad news? We watch killings, murder and children on Amber alert. Can the world live without the drama from our celebrities, Senators, high profile sports stars, Presidents and Congressmen? We have women/men sleeping with our high school students. A perfect example of blind justice.

Has everyone lost their cotton pic-ken mind. Can anyone tell me any different. Good news is a joke. Even going to jail is a celebrated. Talk show host exploit our dirty laundry. Airing our misfortune to the viewing audience to make money.

The good news is that I woke up this morning and I'm alive. The wars and mini bombs plague the head line news. How long should our young soldiers remain in Iraq. Iraq is a country that trains the young to die and even kill their own. Since 911, New York City has not been the same. We are always on high alert. Soldiers heavy presence and security guards at our airports and subways.

The family structure is no longer the typical mother and father. Just baby Mama drama. Kids today learn bad behavior at home. No one wants to make a commitment to one another. It goes in this order: (1) baby after baby with no father (2) live with each other till something goes wrong and separate, (3) no marriage, as this is too complicated today. The lottery money does not go back to the schools as promised.

I'm looking for some good news. Our poor country is getting poorer due to lack of jobs and companies folding due to one reason or the other. Africa is still being robbed of their diamond mines. I'm looking for good news, where child predictors are all castrated. I'm looking for good news that will bring back the lottery money to the schools.

Good news when each person does a good deed and pass it forward. No more bombing and high alerts. No more grown men preying on the young children. Kids in school can learn and become positive adults in the future. Keeping them off the streets. Protect them from bad habits. Good news starts at home. Good news begins and ends with us.

Have You Lost Your Mind

Have you ever felt like you have lost your mine? Everything is going wrong and everyone is out of place. When things are not going your way, your mind is plays tricks with your sanity and you want to tell the world that you are not a moving target. You are not ridiculous. Always feeling surrounded by doubt and uncertainty.

Sometimes I feel lost in a world of misfits and lunatics. Hearing these voices in my head? Tired of listening to them. Going to the doctor to get some relief from the voices. The happy pills take a couple of weeks to help me tread thru the darkness that took hold of my ability to think. Constantly consuming me, thus driving me to the edge. Images of angels taking your hand, bringing you back to reality.

I'm not crazy, just misunderstood. I see thing from a different point of view. Darkness mixed in with the light all the time. I have not lost my mind, just feel like it.

Have I lost my mind? No! Just trying to stay afloat on a sinking ship. Losing your sanity is no joke. So I take it one day at a time.

How can you question my love?—Jessica

How can you fix your lips to question my love. Looking at my little princess for the first time, this bundle of joy. The bundle of joy that filled my heart with unbelievable happiness. Now that you are here, I'm complete. An image of myself looking up to me with those beautiful eyes filled with love. Looking down at you needing my comfort. Promising you at that moment to be the best mother you ever had. No matter what you grow up to be. I will always love you forever.

Can't promise you perfection, nor do I expect perfection from you. Forgiveness goes both ways, there is no handbook on parenting. We learn my trial and error. I can only promise to try my best to understand and nurture you as best I know how. Never giving up on you.

Hoping that our relationship will grow and grow forever. Mother and daughter till the end of time. There will be days that we get on each others nerves but that is to be expected. But lets talk it over. Come hold my hand and make peace not war.

Compromising will help mend our differences. Talking it thru till we come to an agreement. Listen to me honey, I'm trying to make you see that a mother's love should never be questioned. Rest your head on my shoulders my little princess. Sweet dreams I bestow on you each night. I'll be the mother hen to the end. Just believe my love is the real deal Jessica.

To. Don Forman
How Do I Help You Grieve

How do I help you thru this most difficult time? I can't tell you not to cry. Grief is a process leading you back to healing. Don't do what others think you should do or say. Go thru your sorrow your way. Let it go. Scream, yell or get on your knees and pray.

Grief can take you to a very dark place. A place of long suffering. A place where emptiness takes over your well being. A heathen, choking, smothering, don't care life. Only time can heal that womb. Let it all out and don't hold back the tears. Don't try to hold on to that pain. This is part of the process of letting go.

Just know I'm here for you. Wishing that I could take that walk down that lonely road with you. I won't rush you, take as much time as you need to heal. Soon in time with help from family and close friends you will start your healing process.

Sitting across from you, watching the tears roll down your cheeks, powerless, not knowing what it would take to ease this gut wrenching pain you now feel. Trust me, I am not moving. I will watch over you. I want to be the one you can call on if you need too. From the heart, I stand before you to console you and wrap my arms around you. Holding you till you say let go.

Remember, I'll stand by you, till you come out from that dark place.

Can't See

Not being able to see what's in front of me. I only feel the depression that has taken over me. The dark cloud that covers me. I can't get out from under the dark cloud. Everyone sees a different me. They see a strong black women with only strength and courage. When I look in the mirror I can only see an empty void in my face. Life has been a real challenge.

Trying to be what everyone thinks I should be. Trying to be a good person, trying to care. I know that things could be worse. I have a home with a roof over my head. I've come a long way. A tough young girl who grew up as a tomboy, strong and sassy. I had great friends, who were loyal to me.

Still I sit here in the dark and it's cold. Can't see my way through. Hoping this day will go well. I did not shed a tear. If everyone could hear the voices in my head as I try hard to hide the nastiness inside. I'm not well. The confusion, self doubt causing me to crash. Feeling the wind as I fall. The fall so fast and hard.

Sometimes I don't know what to do. I'm anger and confused in my head. Once again I stand in front of the mirror, it's staring back at me. I don't see what other people see. Can I get past this roller coaster ride of depression and the screaming in my head? No future and no past. I see the bad all the time. The happiness is lost in my head, because the voices are getting louder and louder in my ears. The voices are real, the words confusing me all day long. Running and running to no where, no roads ahead. I'm trying to explain what I see and feel. Prayer and a song is the only thing that helps me make it thru each day. Don't feel sorry for me, because one day the cloud will go away. I will be happy. I will one day enjoy the world and feel the happiness that is surrounding me.

I Know That God Loves Me

I know that God loves me.
When the sun hits my face.
When the rain falls to the earth, it's just his way of cleaning away the dirt.
So many things I've prayed for. He gives no more or less than what we need. Maybe not when we ask, only when we least expect it.

I know that God loves me.
When God scratches his head he causes the snow to fall on us.

I know that God love me!
So much crime and sadness in the world.
That's not what he wanted for us. He gave us a brain so that we can make our own mistakes. Hopefully, learning from each and every one we make.

I've paced the floors crying all day in desperation—asking you dear God to give me an answer. Show me the way back to reality.

I know that God loves me!
I woke up today because of you. I've taken another breathe today because of you. You built us a wonderful world in which to live. Gave us common sense to know right from wrong. He can lead us to righteousness only if we follow his examples.

I know that God love me!
He watches over me day and night. Keeping us safe from all harm.

Even when we brush our teeth and when we shower to cleanse our bodies of our sins.
You do not have to see him—You can feel his presence if you are his child.

God sees our every move. God sees many things before we do. He has a plan, so hold on to your faith. He's there for you. I know God loves me because I can feel him from the top of my head to the tip of my toes. Amen.

Need

I need a chance to breathe.
I need a chance to breathe, the darkness so thick and no one can see me.
I need a chance to sing so that I CAN BE HEARD by millions.
I need a chance to fly so that I can see the world.
Things have changed so much in the world, that I'm afraid I will just disappear.
What I need is a safe place a comfort zone.
No crime, just peace.

If I Knew Why?

If I knew why my mind is working on overtime. Why I'm so confused and stressed. People so overworked that they can't see straight. If I knew why your anger came on so sudden. Why is crime up and bliss is blind. The negativity comes so easy and the positive gets lost in the shuffle.

Working 60 hours instead of 40, what a mess.
Trying to pick up the kids, clean the house and pick up the clothes from the dry cleaners. Multitasking is a daily routine. When you're at work you're thinking, "what will I make for dinner or did I turn of the stove?" Everything, is rolling like a bowling ball down the alley.

Living has become a routine. Work, home, shower and then to sleep. Enjoyment is few and so far in between. Romance and play time is a thing of the past. Looking for a way to relax, read a book or compose a song.

Parents are stressed and the kids are happy, not a worry in the world. Parents are trying to have moment to themselves. Nights out with friends have becomes home paying bills. I don't know why things are so hard. We are all pulled in different directions our heads spinning all the time.

Do you know why, the good get stomped on and the bad seems to have all of the fun. Living is like a game of ping pong. Backward and forward the life goes on. It's like taking two steps forward and one back. A never ending cycle.

Take a timeout, just take a deep breathe. Life's too short to always say what if? Enjoy the moment and let the world spin without you, you're not missing anything.

Go the distance and say "stop!" Play hookie, relax, let joy in your life. Take a vacation and enjoy the moment. Take a good hard look at your child. Let them grow up to tell their children about the wonderful times they shared with their parents.

Jessica's Blue's

Don't know why you are disagreeable?
Don't know what made you so sad?
Our home was not that bad.
You did not try, we could have worked this out.

You left before we had a chance to talk it out.
So many things I wanted to say.
I love you with all of my heart.
Needing to understand you.

I know things were not perfect and I you knew that too.
I not going to say that it was all my fault.
I'm just going to say our relationship was a hot mess.
You never wanted to reach out to plea for a solution to our problems.

I just needed more time to fix whatever was ailing you.
You never tried to reach out to me to make peace.
We never had that chance to climb that mountain together.
We could have stopped for a rest together.
I will never give up, no matter what you say or do.
I am waiting and willing to accept your apology with open arms as any good mother would do.
No holding grudges.

Jessica, understand that you will always have a home here.
A warm and cozy bed awaits you.
No more blues—just love in my heart for you.

Keeping Your Sanity

Kill the notion that I'm crazy.
Exile to a place, when you're all alone.
Expect everyone to hear their own thoughts.
Pressure of life getting overwhelming.

Yelling and screaming but no one is there.
Out of control, driving real fast—off the cliff I go.
Under a rock—digging my way out.

Silence your inner thoughts, keeping the enemy inside.
Aliens have taken control.
Noise is too loud can't hear yourself think.
Isolated with nowhere to go
Telling yourself it will get better.
You're the only one—the true judge. Keep your sanity before
you go crazy.

Life Is Too Short

We take so much for grated, family, jobs and just life in general. So many people are self-absorbed. Can we all just be nice and appreciate the moment. So many people are homeless and have died from cancer or HIV.

Focus on the life you are given. Life can be over in just a split second. No notice given. Accidents happens to the good and the bad people, there are no exception to the rules. Waking up each and every day is a gift of life.

Wake up and water the lawn because the grass is not always greener on the other side. Reap the fruits of your labor. Put a smile on your face. Live your life to the fullest. Follow the rules of life. Live with the misery and the hardship and believe that it will get better sooner. This is only a test that we have to pass in life. Life is a struggle. It's your choice to make life hard or easy.

Live your life. Learn from your life. Life is too short. Give life a kick in the ass and go down fighting!!!!!!

Light

The light, the light—so far away. Can't see the end of the tunnel. A captive for far too long. Out of touch with the world and awaiting to submerge from this trap. Not able to keep in touch with things. Wanting to breathe the fresh air once more. Wanting to feel the wind on my face. Wanting to run not walk to get to the other side. Help me reach the end of the tunnel.

Almost there, I find myself screaming out loud. Afraid to make that leap into the light.

Finally, I emerge from this tunnel of darkness. Able to see the light again and feel the sun on my face. Very overwhelmed by my new found freedom. Now able to run thru the forest, roll in the beautiful green grass, climb the highest tree, look at something so simple as the insects crawling on the ground underneath my feet, smelling the scent of the flowers, hearing the birds sing, and playing in the sand. Finally, I get to see the world once more in a different light.

So beautiful, I cried. I'm so happy for the first time in many years.

Free from the sadness and the depression that hovered over me like a dark cloud. Able now to hold my head up high and not afraid of the dark. At the end of that tunnel was my start of a new beginning. Darkness gone never to submerge again. I've found the light again.

For now and always I will be able to enjoy life as it was intended to be. Ready to receive all the blessings that awaits me.

Light that I thought I'd never see. Light, light, so bright has come back to me tonight.

"I'm free at last".

Listening To The Voice Within

When the little voice within speaks, you should listen. When that gut screams out go with it. Your gut feelings never lies, it sends out a signal so strong you cannot ignore. Be aware of the people and your surrounding always. It's funny how the little voice within can save you over and over again or the angel that always sitting on your shoulder.

You will never go wrong if you trust your instincts. The worst decisions are always made in haste. A well thought out plan is best. If it doesn't feel right . . . . run. Better safe than sorry. Listen to the voice within, that indicator tells you something is about to go wrong. So when your gut speaks listen.

I'm alive today because of my inner voice. That inner voice kept me out of trouble plenty of times. Most criminals who ignored that gut feeling wound up in jail or in trouble with the law because they ignored that voice within. My gut guided me through life and opened many a positive door. Listening to the voice within kept me afloat and has never let me down.

Looking For Peace

Sometimes I feel like happiness is so far away. Always trying to find the silver lining. Falling in the lake, I can not swim. No safety net to catch me when I fall. Looking for peace in a crazy world. Dealing with the rage that follows me, strangling and chocking the life out of me. I've fallen down the rat hole, now I'm a meal. Haters all around me, just waiting for me to fail. I'm not going to give in.

So much drama in the world. Even the news—should be called bad news all the time. Bad news sells. Hell on earth is where we live the only safe place is one's mind.

It seems that everyone is out for themselves. Striving for peace in a world that is so crazy, full of wars we cannot seem to end. Sometimes I must admit that I do give up but I retrace my steps and pick up from there to make it right. Felling my heart with happy thoughts and keeping my good friends close.

Looking for peace should be easy but you and I know that it's not.

I'm Looking Thru The Looking Glass

I'm on the outside looking at the world and it's a fascinating place. People, places and things are so vast and wide. The news is never ending. The population has increases ten fold. If you hold the world, in all it's the glory you will see, so many faces and people of all colors like the rainbow.

I'm staring at the world and how it has changed from education to technology. The kid's today surf the internet of knowledge. The technology has advanced. Next, we will have robots cooking and teaching our children. Hopefully, this will never take place because our children of today need guidance and spiritual help.

The weather so crazy from our ozone layers is melting our ice caps. Crazy tornados and high tides. We also need to save our forest and the animals that are being destroyed. No more fur coats or killing our elephants for their tusks. Only eating what our bodies need. No more over eating and wasting food. I hate when people waste food it really fries my eggs.

Too many people living in homeless shelter or in the streets. These people go hungry for lack of food that we waste without thinking. I wish I could save them all and give them peace. Money has placed the standards of living so high that the middle class are holding on to every last dollar, just to survive. The rich ride the backs of the poor while the poor just scrap by. The scale has tipped and the ship is going down.

Now that we have a newly elected President I hope he can help the world. We all cry for world peace but when will we see it. Let's clean our streets and clean our air. The looking glass is clouded by greed and wealth that is unattainable. When the time comes the glass will clear and the people will appreciate the good that's within our hearts. The world can and will be a good place to live again. We all need to give back and stay focused on the big picture. We have one planet and if we are going to live in it we have to get along and help one another.

Loving You—Loving Me

I'm looking into your eyes and seeing so much in you. The father, lover, friend and teacher. It's funny how the heart works—you can't predict who you will fall in love with.

It's easy to love you because you complete me. Loving me is the hardest. The self-doubt and the impulsive moments that I have. It's hard being parents not knowing if you are always doing the right thing. Not sure that you can always provide the love that your family needs.

Loving you gives me strength and the will to go on. I know it is hard to love me back because of all my flaws and insecurities. Baby just understand we are a team.

Love is not always easy and it gets rough at times. We have to take the good with the bad, go thru our ups and downs because in the end our love will be complete.

Making It Through The Night

How can I make it through the night? If you are calling me all throughout the night? My caller ID is full cause you just keep calling. Turning the ringer off, hoping you catch the hint. Ring, ring, please stop ringing. Don't you know how desperate you seem.

I'm over you, please do the same. You say you are happy, then why do you keep calling me? You make up excuses and create unnecessary problems for me and the kids. I can't jump hoops for you anymore.

You had your chance. I'm changing my number for the last time. Blocking your number. I know the phone company is happy too.

A restraining order has been put in place. Moving to another state. None too soon. I'm not running from you, just need some quite from you. You have caused me to uproot for the last time. No more uncomfortable moments for me and the kids. Aren't you tired of making a fool of yourself.

Your new family must be wondering why you are putting us thru this. Now that I have moved, you can no longer tell your new family that I am harassing you. Can you explain to them why you are still fighting with me long distance?

A new year has passed, you should plan a fresh start. Cleanse your heart of the bitterness you have in your heart. We have gone on with life. No more hurt and pain.

Manny

You are my best friend and I don't deserve you. For more than 20 years you have been by my side thru thick and thin, shared the good and bad times and I thank you. Eternally grateful and very blessed to have you in my life. You're more than a friend you are my family. You have my back and I yours. You're the rock that keeps my stone wall up. Can't thank you enough and I will always need you by my side.

We just seemed to click from the very first moment we saw one another. Lady luck found us and brought us together forever. Things happen for a reason my brother. Along the way we met Rey and Sheila. Rey and Sheila became the cement in the stone wall. You three made me a better person and put some sanity in my crazy world.

There were times in my life when I was spinning out of control, you three took hold of the steering wheel and keep me on the road. I've fallen and you guys held the net to catch me each time. You have believed in me and never doubted me. I'm lost for words and a tear have fallen from my eyes not from pain but from all the joy a woman like me could ever have.

I'm here for you now and always. If I had a million dollars to give it would be yours. From this life time to the next, I'll need you. Your friendship and love keeps me afloat.

Missing Child Of Mine

Missing child of mine, "Where are you?" Wondering the streets with no place to go. Don't you know that we miss you and want you to come back home. My thoughts are of you each and every moment of the day. Where are you my child? Please come home. I pray for God to keep you safe from all harm.

Whatever ails your heart we can fix it. You are mad now but that too will pass. There are so many bad people out there ready to prey on you, my beautiful girl. Losing sleep and not eating because I'm missing you. Wondering where you are.

I know in your mind you think that you are doing the right thing, saying to yourself, "I can make it on my own". Did you forget that you need money to stay alive out there all alone. I always wonder where you are sleeping when the darkness comes. These streets are full of so many young girls like you becoming prey to the perverts. These men will say or do anything to get a piece of your ass. A pimp will use you as his mule. A drug dealer will have you strung out, making you sell for him to get your fix.

Please don't fall for the games that people play in the streets. Remember, you don't get something for nothing. There is always strings attached to the money that is handed to you out there. Nothing from nothing leaves nothing my child. Stupidity is no excuse for falling into a trap. Keep you eyes open. Try to find your way back home. We are waiting for you with open hearts. Ready to tuck you in a nice warm bed for the winter. Lots of love waiting for you all year round.

Run away child running wild, please come home tonight. I'm waiting for that knock at the door. Come on in, we can work this out. The family is missing you.

Thinking Of You Mom—Thinking Of You

Mom—I'm thinking of you all the time. Thinking of the good times we shared. Don't remember any bad days. I'm hoping that I've told you that I love you each and every day.

Each day that my head rose up from my pillow meant another day of being with you, my best friend. You taught me all my clean habits—"Brush your teeth once you arise—wash your body and hair—clean your surroundings". The two of us leaving the house each day was a loving moment as you tied my shoes and put my coat on.

Now as an adult with a family of my own I'm missing you so much. Miles has separated us. Sitting here alone at the table drinking something as simple as a cup of tea I could not help think of how you enjoyed yours with two(2) sugars and cream. Thinking of how as a child we strolled hand and hand while taking our walks thru Central Park, in New York City.

Before going out of the door for work you packed a bag for our trips to the park so that after my play and running around with my friends you could change my dirty clothes. The bag was packed with snacks in case I got hungry. All of this love for an only child like me. No competition, no sharing of love with any other kid, just me. Remembering your beautiful long brown hair.

You never missed any special events in my life. Always arriving early so that you could sit in the front row so that I could see that you where there for me. I was special. Even going to the doctor was an assuring trip because you would look into my eyes and say, "It's okay baby."

Off to college, counting the days that I could come home on break. To my surprise on one of those breaks you had dyed your hair black. That was a horrifying moment for me. I had to accept this change because you are still my loving mom.

My love for you is deeper than the deep blue sea.
Love you mom.

The Move

The boxes, the wrapping, the moving of the heavy furniture, the rental of the truck and packing up all the clothes, shoes, the dishes and the pots and pans. Up and down the stairs not knowing when it would all end. Sweating and aching, wishing it were done already.

The move is for the better. Making a fresh start, applying fresh paint to the walls, cleaning to make the air fresh. Empty rooms to be filled. Hoping for a sunny day so that the furniture does not get ruined.

Moving is a bitch and that is no lie. Can't hire a professional mover. Can only rely on good friends and family to help get this done. Wishing that everything could just fall magically into place.

The day has come to an end. Everything has been put away. Can I have a glass of beer or some lemonade?

Looking on the positive side of this move. Our family will have a fresh start. Making room for new memories and hoping for a better life.

My Brother Rey's Birthday Wish!!

I have always admired you my brother. You are my hero. You've never let me down. Tickling my stomach to make me laugh, wiping my tears from my face when I was sad. What can I give a man that has given me so much love?

From the day I was born you stood guard over me. Such a powerful role to undertake. What can I give to replace all that comfort and security you have given me? In a world so full of turmoil, it's nice to have someone like you.

As the years have slipped by, you have helped to mold me into a honest and well rounded young woman. Keeping me out of harms way.

After pondering over and over again in my head as to what to give you. Scratching my head, leaving no stones unturned I finally, decided what to give you for your birthday.

I will wrap up the world with all it's splendored things, tie a bow around it to give to you on your birthday. That's my gift to you.

My Buddy

My Buddy was taken from me at a young age. As a child I laid on his chest and listened to his heart dance. I've grown to love you over the years. Buddy my uncle and my hero. Just as soon as the sun rose and the sky cleared a storm erupted and clouded my days. You went away and that was the last time I looked into your face. Years went by. Nightmares followed. Where is my Buddy.

A father's stricken grief pursued after so much time from Buddy (his son). "Help my son. He's innocent, set him free!" Justice was blind, saying he was innocent fell on deaf ears. An innocent man was put away for a crime he did not commit. Lawyers, churches and family stood by his side. Before he was exonerated by justice, his father had died. Buddy was not able to attended his funnel and this compounded his grief. New lawyers and new evidence set him free. His father would never know that he was eventually freed.

As a child I remembered you well, but as time passed your face had faded. Now as an adult with children of my own, I sat watching T.V, low and behold there you were. Standing tall and a free man set free in Kentucky. As I listened to the story and your name flashed across the screen "William T. Gregory" a free man, at last DNA has cleared his name.

I screamed and yelled "that's where you have been all these years." My mother's twin. In spite of all the suffering you had been thru in jail you were still a handsome man. A monetary settlement was awarded. Money will never compensate you for the mental anguish and stress you had to endure.

Spend the money wisely my Buddy cause you will never know when another stormy day will come again. I send you my prayers and love to keep your heart strong. Much love from me to you.

Your Loving Niece, Sabrina Gregory

My Three Days

It's funny how our little time together flew by. Our three day weekend was not enough. The minutes and the hours just flew by. You working all the time did not allow us enough time to play together or make plans for relaxation.

Can I make anyone understand what we are up against? Having to sneak off in some corner of the house to be alone. No time to enjoy each others company. So little time, so little time, trying to enjoy the little fun left of this sunny day out with the family.

Being in a bigger place now and still can't escape. The three day weekend gave us a little time to talk with one another over the dinner table. We planned a candlelight dinner with a little wine. Having an extra day with one another may not seem like much but it was better than nothing. We have to do something to keep the sparks flying.

My man works nights but he would like very much to change to days. Day work would allow him to come home after a hard days work, take a shower, sit down to the dinner table with us every night, allow the two of us to go to sleep at the same time, waking up in the morning in each others arms, talk for awhile during the day and maybe take a short drive or just hang out with one another before the kids come home from school.

I know his job is important and the money he makes pays the bills but I can't help but wish that he could be home for me to enjoy. Wishing our life was somewhat like Adam and Eve swinging through the jungle with no cares in the world.

The three day weekend, eating breakfast, have lunch at noon, dinner at six, watching the late night show with Johnny Carson, making love and falling asleep together is all a part of my wish.

Night Owl

I'm a night owl and I can't sleep. Working during the night and sleeping during the day hours. The work sucks but it pays the bills. I feel like a vampire working the night shift. Daytime for me does not come. The work sucks but it pays the bills. Can anyone please give me a raise. So tired my body hurts, yet too tired to sleep. I've worn a sleeping mask to simulate the dark, tried sleeping pills but that's not good—one can become addicted to sleeping pills. Can't sleep can anyone help me? I just want to sleep, everyone needs to understand how hard it is to work the night shift.

The bill collectors and solicitors keep calling. Tired of hanging up but to no avail they keep calling. Can't shut off the phone as there be an emergency call. If I could change my shift I would. The night differential is great. Don't know what to do. OOH, OOH, says the owl when it speaks, who the hell started this thing. So we take the good with the bad. That's what I'm saying.

Okay, if I could change my shift I would. However, I would not benefit from this. I'm a family man and the family needs me to provided the best. It's hard to function on three hour of sleep every day. Almost passed out taking my kids to school. So I drink a lot of coffee and the caffeine is going too my head. If the caffeine from the coffee does not work, I switch to Red Bulls that kicks in right away. It gives me wings alright and when the caffeine wears off so do I. Crashing so hard I feel like someone that is falling from an airplane into the obese.

Owl of the night on the train. Home by 2 A.M. My wife is just turning over, hopefully, her dreams are good. She is a stay at home wife and she is overworked with no pay. In charge of the house, kids and her nap is her only break. We have a good relationship because we trust one another and that's a good thing. Only night owl's understand each other's pain.

The real benefit's the sacrifices that are made for your family makes you feel tall and this lets you know that you are the man that your family depends on. Set a date on the calendar for a family day. Then turn off the clock for a sleep in on the weekend. Night owl's are hard working people who are just tired and need a break.

My First Born

Let me bestow my love and protection upon you my beloved child. No sadness do I want to see in those beautiful eyes my little warrior? Let me fight your battles, no worries—no tears. Mommy will protect you. Just play and do all the natural things that a child does. Just play be carefree just let me help you to grow up full of joy and pride. Be a great man full of wisdom, respect and loyalty to manhood.

Nine Lives

Just like a cat with nine lives. I have scratched and pawed and fought many battles. Fought till I could not stand to be victorious in life. Hopefully, this struggle will allow me to see another day. God bless me and my family every time we open our eyes.

The Obstacle

The worst thing about not knowing is waiting. Not seeing the future, fear of the unexpected. I've been on the receiving end of this fear for years. Waiting and waiting always waiting. I'm always saying "only me", because the unexpected and the worst things in life always happened to me. I've endured so many obstacle, trials and trivializations. If those obstacles does not kill you they will certainly make you a stronger person. My body feels like a train running uncontrollable on a short track headed for a wreck. Running scared and trying to beat the odds. Not going to be beaten by life an it's many trap's. Life's a bitch then you grow up. Not going to be beaten by life and it's many traps. So much that I have to accomplish. Trying to be wise in my old age. Trying to make a difference in my life and in my mind. Just living is not an option.

Where do I start? Do I start at the middle or somewhere in between. Can't blame God, for my choices. We choose our own path. Whether it's good or bad. The roads are sometimes rocky with lots of tricky turns. Can I drive on this road or do I stop for help (need directions.) I hate to lose and I WILL GET THE LAST WORD! I've fallen on hand times and can't get up. We all need help every now and then to get on the right path.

Keep your head above water and let life run it course. Can't run from the challenges or the bumps in the road. One needs to stand and fight those small battles in order win the war. Sometimes I feel like I'm drowning in sorrow and pain. No pain killers taken just straight up pain. The pain in constant and hard. Can I get some help here? I need a tall knight—to help me take that smooth ride on his horse to salvation. To no avail that knight has passed me by.

To set the record straight, I must make a stand and be brave. Face all my demons. Real life is about ups and downs and I am determined to beat it. Going to make myself strong and take my life back. Be a HERO to myself. Take control and move forward from this day forth.

Top Of The World

Don't be so cocky when you are on that high,. It's head or tails when you are rolling the dice. One day that luck will run out. Are you ready for that fall?

I don't even remember when luck began or ended for me. The luck just ran out. The shit just hit the fan. I don't know what I did in another life to deserve such bad luck and misfortune. Has God forsaken me? Rich people who sit on top of the world just don't understand how people like you and me are living from day to day, wondering where their next meal is coming from.

On top of the world—when that luck comes without merit you became a wheel spinning out of control. That axle from that wheel will break. You either dust yourself off and strive to do better or become one of those people that thinks they cannot coupe and commit ultimate sin. Taking your life. Thus, left in limbo between heaven and hell.

Top of the world is state of mind. You make or break your luck. Only you can change your destiny of today and tomorrow. Strive to be the best you can be always.

Sipping On Gin and Juice

Life looks good when you are looking thru the red eyes of that alcohol glass and feeling like you are on top of the world. A perfect example of that gin and juice is; the story of the little old lady that lived in a shoe, with so many children, she did not know what to do. She was just plastered out of her mind. No one knew. Sometimes a little gin does not hurt. Don't get drunk every night just when it's necessary **LIKE:**

When you lose your job.
Have too many kids and not enough money.
You just found out that your wife has cheated on you again.
When bankruptcy is not an option but a necessity.
The teenage kids has crashed the second car this week.
Divorce happened for the third time.
When you wife says she's pregnant with quintuplet.
When you have to work three job just too eat.
When after the child support is paid and the money left can only buy you one drink.

When life throws you a lemons make a Long Island ice tea and call it a day.

Sitting Here Waiting

Sitting here feeling helpless and uneasy, no one is checking to see if you are okay.

Watching you sleep, looking like an angel. Looking at you reminds me of when I was a child, always looking up into the face of someone I loved. Feeling so happy that someone was there for me.

For the duration of your young life, my little baby girl, I will stand tall and strong like an armored guard by the wall.

Sitting here waiting to make sure all your needs are met. Making sure you know that I love you with all my heart and soul.

I will sit here till the end of time. Being your guardian angel throughout the night.

Sitting here waiting for an answer from the nurse because your heart is ill. Nurses all around your bed, checking your I.V. and distributing your meds as needed throughout the night. Hoping your heart will be alright.

I love you so much even when you get mad because this too shall pass. Your feeling means a lot to me.

Sitting here waiting like I should each and every day doing what all good moms do. Holding on to hopes of your getting well. Numb and sore from sitting. Sitting here waiting for the doctors to say you are OK.

Once you have healed. I will hold you close. Never letting you go. What a scary moment this has been for us both.

Sliding into 1ˢᵗ Base

If you think about it, life is like a sliding into first base. You're either safe or out. Being on top of the world gives you the same feeling as that home run you made. Making the best decisions in this world is like sliding into home plate watching the cheers on your teammates faces. Crowds jumping out of their seats. Here goes the tension, "two men on base, you're coming up to the plate, in your mind you have to make a double play or swing that bat hard enough to make at least one run in".

Looking back at the coach telling you to make a sacrifice play. Do you heed his advice to bunt? Yes/no. Life is full of decisions, decisions, decisions.

On the field and trying to get to that homerun can feel like rush hour, dodging, weaving, and bobbing thru traffic until that cop pulls you over to hand you that speeding ticket.

Slide into 1st base is a metaphor of life. Concur, step up to the plate, make that home run to victory, be the hero of the game.

Someone Always Watching

In a places where people are just strangers too one another, there is always someone watching. Privacy is a thing of the past. From the Paparazzi to the National Enquirer. The lives of the rich and famous dominating the T.V screens and the news is always bad. Things are not good when you have someone following you around exploiting your life to make a buck or two. We don't live in glass houses but somehow, someway, some where, someone out there finds a way to get the dirt on you to air and misfortune to the public. That once well kept secret is no longer yours. Your secret is now the headline news broadcasting your shame.

We live in a cruel world that is looking to take your freedom. Simply watch your back. Take no ones kindness for weakness. Stand up tall and hold your head up high, never let the next man take your spot. I know it sound rough but I'm a paranoid sister who's been around the block a few times. Keep your friend close and your enemies even closer. Keep your eyes on the golden ring ahead and don't let anyone cause you to lose track of what's important in your life. Eye for an eye and punch the next guy in the teeth. But when the eyes are all looking you have to be prepared.

Someone is watching all the time. Don't fall asleep on the job, because there is a long line at the unemployment office. A staving man is ready to take your plate away from you, so watch your back.

My Spanish Harlem

When I was a young girl, I lived in a place called Spanish Harlem in New York City. Beautiful blue skies above us at night. My Spanish Harlem was the bomb. Dominicans and Puerto Ricans ruled the turf from 110th street to 112th street. The Puerto Rican Day parade was the long awaited event that was shared by all. The festival was celebrated by both Dominicans and Puerto Ricans. The one of the few times both culturals united together for a good time of fun, laughter, enjoyment of food and good music to dance by. So many things have changed.

The Corsi House which was once a great dollar movie house on 116th street has been torn down. Many Chuchifrito's are gone. The Marqueta which stretched from 110th to 116th street is also gone. This market helped feed the poor neighborhood. The cheap meats and vegetables could feed an army. High rise condo's forced the poor out because they could not afford to live there anymore.

Now Spanish Harlem is filled with Mexican's that took over. No beef with them. It's just that they took over so fast. Nothing remained the same. My high school, Manhattan Center for Science and Math was changed drastically. The old Jefferson pool and park has empty basketball courts and the pools are dry. Even the Italian Feast able has been reduced to a small block with limited rides for the kids. The Pizzeria and the Italian restaurants are still standing.

Changes due occur, memories never fade. Spanish Harlem is just a good memory that I shall never forget.

Star Light

Looking into the night sky, feeling the breeze so cool on my face. Making a wish tonight. May the universe hear my cries. Star light so bright, may the world hear me tonight. The night sky is clear and the man in the moon is awake. Star light so bright I need sunglass tonight.

Stars are so bright, grant me this wish for everyone out there that has fallen on hard times, bless them with wealth and wisdom. Enough money to get them all over the hump. A comfortable home not a mansion. Money for peace of mind and happiness.

Star so bright grant this wish for everyone and me tonight. Luck given to the true believer. I'm just trying to get a piece of the pie for needy people and me tonight.

Starting Shit!

You are starting shit with me again. I'm not going to go there with you anymore. For all these years I've tried to reason with your but your ignorant ass won't budge. If you were not the father of my kids, I would have nothing to do with your ass. I've tried reasoning with you, never raising my voice above a whisper. Our kids do not have to get involved in this mess.

Now after thirteen years of bickering back and forth, you want to have a reasonable conversation. "Why?" Money has entered the equation. Getting into your pockets got your attention I'm not feeling sorry for you and I won't cry you a river. There is no shame in your game and now there is none in mine.

I'm not beating around the bush or covering up for you anymore. Not telling the kids lies in order to keep the peace in the family. Hiding your lack of support for them. I should have seen this coming from the beginning. All the signs were there. My love for you blinded all your short comings. I must have been out of my mind to think you would change in time. Always fighting about the things that should have stayed in the past.

After thirteen years of being divorced you are still fighting, worse than a woman scorned. Stop bitching, suck it up, take your licks and keep on stepping out of my life. Be a father to your kids.

Stop the lawyers and the fees. We are no longer married or bound to one another anymore. Move on and enjoy your new supposedly happy life. I'm not going there with you anymore. It's time for you to move on. Stop the shit.

Summer Time Fun

The kids are out of school and some of the teachers stay around to help those kids that have make up classes. No fun for them. The parks are full of life. Out of all the four seasons I think we all love the summer time because the sun is shinning bright upon our faces and the days are longer. The kids can stay up all night long and sleep in the next day. Just love the summer time. The ice cream trucks come by every day, kids can turn on the water pumps to play and get wet in order to cool off. Families plan vacations and the flowers are in full bloom.

On the flip side of summer time—criminals, sexual perverts and drug dealers are there to make money by trying to entice our innocent kids that are just trying to play and have fun. The parks are open late and muggers love that. The trains are packed with tourist. But the cops stay on high alert alone with the National Guards both trying to stop the immigrants at the boarder of these United States.

Summer time allows our kids to have a great time. Kids no longer have to study for those tests. My kids go to Florida to stay with their dad. Just like some kids that will spend some time with the absent parents in their lives. Giving them a chance to see if the grass is greener on the other side.

Summer camps is also great. Summer camp helps us to keep our kids out of trouble. Can things get any better? For the days that it's too hot the pools and lakes are another source of fun for our kids. The beaches become packed with the sunbathers and the surf is up for the surfer dudes.

Getting into top shape is on their minds. Grilling outdoors. All type of outdoor fun. Picnicking sounds nice too.

I'm so happy that summer is finally here so the we can fish, boat, hike and have a great time together. Summer time is here for now so let is eat, drink and be happy.

The Demons Within

It's funny how this good, bad and ugly world has become so hard to live in. It's hard for a good person to stay honest. So much drama. Keep the demons away by surrounding yourself with positive people. Get rid of the negative elements in your life. Too much confusion to deal with. Just like life, you have the devil on one shoulder and the angels on the other shoulder. Don't let the demons in. Stay strong.

When there is a battle going on within think of it as a potato. Smash it and make mashed potatoes out of it. Challenges in life are always there no matter how hard we try. Don't follow the weak. Follow the strong people, listen to what your gut feelings are telling you.

The demons within are taking over our kids also. Tempting them to follow the wrong crowds. Keep your kids grounded at all time. They only imitate you and what they see you do. Set a good example for them to follow. Stay on top of the game, go to work, pay your bills on time, stay faithful to your spouses, let those demons take a back seat in your life. Spend quality time with your family.

Demons are everywhere. Don't let the demons take over.

The meaning Of Sex For The Sexiest

For women sex is a meaningful expression between two people who love one another

For men sex is a way to get their rocks off. Once that 2 second thrill is over they go on their merry way home.

Men visualize having a threesome, only if they can talk you into it.

Women love good passionate sex.

For men good or bad sex is better than none.

Women get all dolled up. Buying the sexiest lingerie to spice up the romance.

Men's version on eye appeal is with his penis.

Foreplay for women is the appetizer before the meal that needs to be tasted and enjoyed slowly.

Men's foreplay is, "Lets it get is on."

Women love long walks on the beach and intelligent conversation.

For a man the long walk is from the living room to the bedroom with very little conversation on the way.

Females think about the future like: "where is this relationship going." Trying to make the ride easier.

A man's mind just wonders, "what can you do to get him off."

The beginning of a relationship for women is romance and hoping to get closer to that man in her life.

For the man the beginning of a relationship is a race to the bedroom only to take your panties off.

When the man dumps the woman he will not give you a reason why it's over.

The woman wants to know why and what did she do wrong. " Maybe I can I fix this," she says.

The man calls you, stalker and he's ready to get a restraining order out on your ass.

The love notes and messages left before on your answering machine telling you all the things you want to heart, melting your heart has now ceased.

Your constant phone calls and notes has made this man run. I mean run as fast as he can.

Women wait to hear those magic three words, "I love you."

This same man will answer, "Get down on your knees bitch."

A woman is always trying to change her man

While the man just wants the woman to pleasure him.

This is the meaning of **sex for the sexiest**.

The Numbers Game

I've heard the answers at least ten times. The seventh month on the seventh day of the seventh year is suppose to be a lucky day. Nine, one, one gets the police attention. Four, one, one gets questions answered. Nine eleven will be a horrible memory for all New Yorker's forever. The numbers game gave different answers to different questions for different people in different place.

Six, six, six, is the devils lucky day and lucky numbers. Women often hide their age, while men become more distinguished as they age. We humans have ten fingers and ten toes, as dogs have four paws. When going to a casino the numbers are your best friend and your enemy on the craps table.

Turning twenty one is great, while turning sixty you are all worn out and ready to retire. Funny, so many numbers meaning so many different things at different times and different moments of our lives. Your sweet sixteenth birthday is celebrated, what a joyous moment. Twenty five, oh man, become legal able to drink yourself to death. So many numbers and my favorite is January eighth, nineteen sixty eight at ten minutes to eight on a Sunday morning. The day of my birth. First time I opened my eyes outside my mothers womb.

I've often wondered what the world would be like without numbers. How would we count the days and years ahead. Mark space and time. Can we mark the number of times we wake up to go to work? The numbers game is the way everyone of us keep track of our daily lives.

I'm thinking of a number from one to infinity. Can you guess that number? I have four children ranging from ages two to sixteen years old. My fiancé and I have known each other for twenty one years. We dated for six years and I can count the number of disagreements we have had on one hand. So, the numbers game goes on and on and on.

The best time is when I wake up each day to my children and family. Kissing them goodnight each night. Those numbers are precious, full of happiness they gave me throughout the years. I hope to celebrate my fiftieth anniversary with the same man. So in my case the numbers game has been played out in my favor. How about yours?

Ten Things I Love About You

Ten things I love about you, let me begin.

The **first** time I every saw you in a crowd.
The **second** I knew that you were the one I wanted to marry.
After our third date we were married on the **third** of June.
When our **fourth** child was born we agreed it was our last.
Five carrot gold ring we shared as a token of our love.
For the **six** hundredth time we said "I love you to one another."
We placed **Seven** candles on top of our first born son birthday cake.
The **eighth** wonder of the world.
I experienced **Nine** years of waking up to your face—Oh what a thrill.
Our **tenth** anniversary has come and we are still together and hoping for many more years to come.

Things I Can Not Change

I can't charge the fact that I have four children or the fact that I'm a divorcee. During the marriage I thought I was in love.

I can't change the fact that in today's world women out number the men. I would love to change that ratio. Bring back peace and tranquility. Cure the many women and men of this deadly disease called, **AIDS**.

I can't change the racial tension in the world but I would like to help change the word, I can't. Trying to be realist about my life—not holding on to anything that is out of my reach. When you say you never will, you set limitations in your life. Be positive and live a better life.

Life is filled with haters full of jealousy. These people don't try to accomplish anything. There job is to discourage you. There is two kinds of people in this world—the haves and the don't have. Which one are you? You can improve that by creating a circle of good people happy thoughts and positivity—never turn your back and on the haters.

Don't let negativity stop you from achieving your goals. Be yourself and don't be a follower, be a leader.

I know that I can change myself and the choices that I make in life. Follow the right path, don't make any detours, don't always take the easy road. The easy road is not teaching you anything. Take risks, don't hold back. Don't beat yourself up or give up. Be your own cheerleader and press forward. Change brings about good things in your life.

Thinking Of Something

I'm thinking of my life and I'm not sure if things are going as planned. So many things that I can't do and so many thing that I yet to accomplish.

Life can be as hard as nails at times. Many things has happened that will change my future. Like not finishing college and getting my health back.

I can't complain because so many people never get that one chance to make their lives better. Living in poverty on the streets with no food. Filling an empty drum full of paper and scrap wood to make warmth on those long cold winter nights. Just thinking of how it would feel to be in a warm bed to sleep.

They say, "What doesn't kill you will make you stronger." What if the hard times are so sad that you become buried so deep that you become eternally lost drowning in your own sorrow?

Killing yourself is never an option but living thru the pain is even harder. We find ourselves looking for the light at the end of the tunnel.

I'm thinking of something to help me thru the day. The only thing that keeps me going is my children and my spouse. Waking up to them everyday makes life better. My mom is also an important piece of that waking up because I love her very much and would not want to ever lose her. Family is all I have.

Thinking of something or someone precious in my life gives me something to live for. Thinking of the months and years ahead with them is my survival kit. Making the best of each day and never looking back, never thinking of what I could have, or should have had. Let it all go.

Changing your future for the rest of your life means letting the light shine through. Clear your mind, think positive thoughts only. Letting go of the negativity.

This Old House

The house at the end of the street was empty for a long time. Many people have moved in for short period of time only. They rented and did not respect the house and they trashed the place. Can this house be fixed?

A new family came to see the house. They took a good long look at this house. It needed a fresh coat of paint and the roof leaked. The lawn was dying and needed a rack and some watering.

They decided to take the house not as a renter but owner instead. This would allow them to fix it up and make it livable forever. Now this house has been cleaned and made livable again and put back in tip top shape. They marvel at their hard work. They had to start from the inside out and worked hard each day. They painted, put in new windows and cleaned out the drains. Making improvement day after day.

They took this old house from rags to spectacular, awesome, breathe taking beauty. The neighbors were in aah. They could not believe the improvements that was made to this old house. All it took was patience and tender hard work and loving care.

No one believed that this was the same old dark run down house that was around the corner and down the street. From all these other beautiful homes. So many people had passed it by without seeing it's beauty and luster that was under all that ugly wood. Boarded up windows and sun burned grass due to neglect.

At the end of the cat cove and down the street now lies a wonderful house that just needed love and hugs and tender loving care. I'm the house for this man and he is my love. He taught how to love before it was too late. The love he showed me allowed me to glow again. Can you believe that? I am looking forward to showing myself off, allowing everyone to see me in my glory. This man has made me shine from head to toe.

<u>To My Father</u>

To my father, I offer you my love and gratitude. Because of you I am a better person today.

You're my best friend, my idle and I love you with all my heart. The things I have accomplished has been done because of your guidance.

Out of love and respect I will always thank you over and over again for being there for me.

In a world of strangers you have been my protector.

The strength and courage you provided has made me a stronger person.

This strength you gave will be forever embedded in my heart and soul.

No one has given me so much support. But the funniest part is that it took a great woman to make you my best dad. You're one in a million.

You're the CEO of my home security and master of all my affairs.

From this day forth and every day of my future—You are my Hero.

Love you dad.

I'm Torn

Don't know what to do?
It hurts, can't see thru the fog, so dark and **dreary**.
No one can imagine how darkness can consume one's soul.
Holding onto a person that does not want to be saved.
Can't help you if you don't tell me why you are struggling.
No words just empty inside.
Cold as ice. Hotter than the sun.
Needing to find oneself. Needing to know what what's going on.

I'm torn because I love you so deeply. My love so pure.
As white as the falling snow. I need to know.
Won't give up on you. That's what you think.
You cut me down with silence. No words ever said.
Don't turn you back on me if you want me to stay.
Can't hold you if you leave. Running away does not solve any this.

No emotion, no remorse, just anger and hate.
I'm here with open arms no matter what.
Torn and confused cause you don't love me like you should.
Okay, I understand completely, you are full of anger and hate.
Not seeing the light at the end of the tunnel.
Shutting me out is what you want to do.
I'm sorry that you feel this way, but **I'm** only human, so give me a break.

Bitterness will only stop the healing process and destroy you inside.

Flesh of my flesh, fruit of my loin, you are a part of my quest for good. I've tried to break that stone cold wall you put before us. Closing your heart so as not to feel.
Torn between right and wrong. I'm weak and sore. Why don't you just get over it. Just shoot me and watch we fall. I don't know what you really want to do. Murder will haunt you.
I'm torn because a mothers bond is precious. Wake up and hear the birds sing.

Cleanse your mind of all that hate. Forget about an eye for an eye, or that tit for tat stuff. You're confused, just watch we draw a line in this sand and come over here. If you cross this line, no one will judge you. Just take my hand and we shall begin anew.

What Do Men Want

What do men want?
They don't know. They want a freak behind closed doors and a angel in public.
They prefer drama and hell, instead of peace and love. Men don't want women who will stand by their side thru thick and thin.
They like those yelling, driving them straight to hell and to bankruptcy types.

Men want those high maintenances, Prada wearing, weave wearing, pedicure and manicuring, none cooking, give me money for my light bill, can't clean what have you done for me lately bitches.

What do men want?
Give me, give, me, want, want, want, take, take, and take me too bankruptcy court.

I can cook and clean, do you right, but noooooooo you don't want me. Good girls finish last.
Good girl can't finish first as long as we have weak ass, ghetto plotting, man stealing, don't turn your back, IQ of a turnip, fake tites ignorant heifers all around them.
What do men want? They don't know and I don't care . . . .

What We Do for Love?

What are willing to do for love? Will you overlook your partners faults and imperfections. Things you thought were cute will drive the nail in the coffin. When the love is fresh and new its exciting. The never ending phone calls, the walks in the park, the picnics and the midday movie shows, the closing down the local dinners, the sleepovers, the finishing each other sentences and the thoughts of forever being in love.

Your mates voice sounds like music to your ears thus enhancing your thought of those romantic notions. You receive flowers just because, constant e-mails, the phone never stops ringing, neither one of you wants to hang up, the lovemaking blows your mind, the sparks that seems to last forever.

Listing to the radio and dedicating a love song, celebrating the first kiss and first time we met. Watching the sunsets, swimming naked in the lake, the slightest touch that sends chills down your spine. Love is a wonderful, they make songs about their feelings. Can things get any better? Love turns the heat up in the bedroom. Checking your voicemail just to hear their voice. I'm just one in millions that has felt this wonderful feeling.

If you love being in love then hold on tight to this never ending roller coaster ride. This is just the beginning. Love hurts and bleeds you dry. Love takes control and gives you wings you never thought you had. Love is still baffling at times. Rainbows are always in the sky, the rain never comes. Writing each other names in the sand, craving your initials in the old oak tree. Sending message from across the room. The stars in each other's eyes.

Things could not get any better. The leaving the toilet seat up will drive you crazy but love allows you to ignore it for now. Never letting this feeling fade, always a need to step up the game. Love can go up and down like a roller coaster ride. Keep your eye on the goal you've set for yourselves. Will marriage make us complete? Waking up too your face each and ever day for the next hundred year. Able to pass down our legacy of love onto our kids and great grand kids. The ultimate end just being in love till the end of time.

<u>What Shall I Do?</u>

I don't like it when someone else is in control.
My cash flow is in your hand.
My stay at home house work always done.
Making calls to make sure we are getting the best deals that
are available.

What shall I do?
Staying within a phone call away.
I'm the man when you are away. Taking out the trash and
shoveling the snow.

Cleaning all day is an obsession, from the floors too the walls.
My domain is the four walls and three floors of this house.
What shall I do when thing get out of control?
Have to go where ever you take me.
My living arrangements are in your hands.
Good girl don't complain.

You are lucky that I give you so much power over me.
Don't get it twisted now, I do have a brain. You don't see
that cause you set the rules.

When I get a chance I will be an equal partner. Not a Barbie
doll like I am now, or a trophy wife you set on a shelve.

What shall I do?
Credit card use is only when you say.
Cash is limited and I want a say but you know how to say "No."
Maybe you don't know how controlling you are.

Your line is not bent and everything is not black or white.
You're not color blind, you just don't see. I trust you cause
I need to hold on to the faith.

What shall I do when the ball is in your hands?
I'm not blind, or can't see, I just put all the trust, love and
faith in your hands knowing you are a good man.
I'm not trapped, just a victim of circumstance, not working,
no self esteem. I'm trying not to complain, just make me an
equal partner in you life so that I can breathe again.

When Your Childhood Is Lost

Innocence is a thing of the past. Children are bigger and taller than I remember. The girls are much more aggressive than the boys. Children having babies. Your boys are father by the age of 15. Virginity is not sacred. Can they be lost in the race to become young men and women. What's the big rush?

Children think they know everything. They are busy trying to fit in with gangs or experiment with drugs. They have not yet stopped to think that the future is in their hands. They are our future. Kid's need their childhood in order to enrich their adulthood. So many things to do and see.

Why can't they go to neighbor gym, play stick ball, jump rope, climb trees or just try to make their neighborhood a better place to live. Stop trying to party thru the break of dawn.

It's so hard to raise children in this day and age. Trying to keep up some kind of family values is a joke. The challenge for today's parents are to keep their children grounded—asking them before they leave the house, "where can I reach you, leave a number, are the parents of that house you are going to are visit are at home and be home at a certain hour or you will be grounded?"

Children of today, please remember once your childhood is gone. You do not get a second chance to do it over. It is gone forever.

You Don't Say

If I heard a rumor circulating around you, would I believe it? Will all the years of our relationship be tarnished by one rumor. Would I believe you if you said you are telling the truth or should I go on pure faith? It's really hard to find a good relationship in this day and age. So many people have tried to ruin our relationship.

Twenty years is longer than most marriages. Should I throw it all away or am I going to go on trusting in you. You have been there for me thru thick and thin, thru ups and downs and in sickness and in health. My life has always been in your hands. No one things is going to damage that.

I've learned so much from you. The ultimate bond we have formed means more than one rumor. The devil is truly working overtime on this one. So when the rumor mill did start I replied "You don't say!" If I would have believed them I would has lost more than a good relationship. I would have let them win.

In the end it comes to trust. I trust you my best friend. Over anyone else. Anything worth having has it's ups and downs. This is just another test of fate. Stick to your guns and let it roll over your back. Take a deep breathe and let it ride. This is why we will to friends for life. I say this from the bottom of my heart.

You Suck

You suck and I'm sick and tired of your game.
You lie, you do whatever you want with no regard for
anyone else.

You suck and you make me want to scream.
I just want to choke you till you turn blue in the face.
You suck—you get on my last nerves.
I'm so tired of the lies and deceit.

From now on I'm going to do me because you think only
of yourself.
So you can choke on it and fall off a BIG CLIFF.

I'm Scared

I'm scared because my life is too short, and I'm not living my life to the fullest.
I'm scared because it's time for my children to leave the nest.
I'm scared that I will die before my parents or I will die alone.
I'm afraid of my past mistakes. Afraid the past has ruined by future.

I'm scared that I've lost my daughter's love already but very secure with my three sons love.
My sons love is deeper than the deep blue sea.
I'm afraid that I will stay broke financially but stay rich with love.

Being afraid is a hard way to live.
Just barely existing is even harder.
Being afraid to hold onto a person that does not want to be held.

Loving my parents with all my being gives me joy and happiness. Not being able to help when they need it makes me sad. Each and every one of our children are different. We are parents just hoping that our love is enough.

Rich with love, poor in the pockets but ever so thankful.
Do you think that the rich are really happy?
The material things will come and go but the love of family are forever.
Being afraid will not stop me from living. Taking a leap of faith with God is what I will do!!

I'm Losing My Mind

I'm losing my mind in this crazy world that we live in. Nothing is going my way. Is seems that the rich people start a lucrative business that bears an abundance of fruit thus leaving the world down on its knees. Everything on a silver platter. Meanwhile, the poor live in the world that is literally falling apart at the seams.

We live in a time where teens are killing teens and their babies are literally being thrown out of windows or dumped into the garbage cans. Drugs are killing our youth and leaving this world with fatherless children. The teen generation has no respect for their elders or authority. Crime is a job for them.

Trying to stay sane in this crazy world is an ordeal. Keeping my therapist on speed dial. Going to meetings where the crazy seem normal.

If I'm losing my mind, then the world is not right. The pills I take to keep me in touch with reality is not working. Someone please give me a refill with the maximum dose. Doctors are quick to give you a pill. Even the commercials start by saying "Do you suffer from headaches, dry mouth and so on and so on" we have a pill for you. The drugs industry is doing great right now. They make a pill for whatever ails you.

Losing my mind in a world where promises are made to be broken. Everyone say what you want to hear. Can an answer come soon? I'm losing the battle don't know where sanity begins or where it ends. The doctors are the drug pushers. The government are the guns that sent our young men to die.

Every day in a senseless war that should have never started. Our soldiers should be able to make a sound decision on their own choosing to live or die for our country.

Let's take control—stand up for our rights. Can we get a break? Stay strong in this crazy world in a challenge.

Get Published, Inc!
Thorofare, NJ 08086
08 February, 2010
BA2010039